The Earthly Paradise of

WILLIAM MORRIS

The Earthly Paradise of

WILLIAM
MORRIS

EDITED BY

Clare Gibson

Grange
BOOKS

Published by Grange Books
An Imprint of Grange Books PLC
Units 1–6, Industrial Estate
Hoo, near Rochester
Kent ME3 9ND

This edition published 1999

Produced in association with Saraband Inc.

ISBN: 1-84013-245-0

Printed in China

9 8 7 6 5 4 3 2 1

For Anna Malan and Lucy Wood.

CONTENTS ❧

FOREWORD

*"I am the man that knows, that feels all poetry
and art, that can create, that can sympathize
with every man and woman that ever lived."*

At the age of twenty-two, William Morris (1834–96) wrote prophetically: "My work is the embodiment of dreams in one form or another." He and his associates in the artistic fellowhsip they called "the Brotherhood" passionately espoused the principles of medieval art and craftsmanship, decrying the soullessness of the Industrial Revolution. This antimodernist stance pervaded Morris's work: it was expressed in his romantic poetry, in his campaign for the preservation of ancient buildings, in the artistic experiments of his interior design firm, in the books printed by the Kelmscott Press, and, finally, in his commitment to Socialism. Morris believed that art could not be divorced from the craftsman's living conditions and communal support for his aesthetic. His utopia foresaw a world in which the iniquities of the machine age were conquered by enlightenment and fraternal equality in closely knit communities that resembled the medieval guilds. Like most utopias, his did not materialise just as he had envisioned it. In fact, toward the end of his life he wrote sadly: "Now that I am grown old and see that nothing is to be done, I half wish that I had not been born with a sense of romance and beauty in this accursed age." Yet history has vindicated Morris as an artist of rare accomplishment in many spheres and a towering figure of the Arts and Crafts movement he helped to found. His vision, creativity and humanity are as relevant today as they were a century ago.

OBJECTS
OF
BEAUTY

The
Decorative
Arts

Morris's first artistic collaboration was in 1858, when he created frescoes for the Oxford Union with a group of artists including Dante Gabriel Rossetti and Edward Burne-Jones. These two men were among the key figures in Morris's "Firm"—Morris, Marshall, Faulkner & Co., which was founded in 1861 to create high quality textiles, wallpapers, tapestries, stained glass and furniture. Today Morris is best known for the medievalist style that he cultivated in the decorative arts, and for his emphasis on motifs inspired by nature. As W. B. Yeats observed in November 1896, "He was a prophet; and it was his vision of that perfect life...that awakened every activity of his laborious life—his revival of medieval tapestry and stained glass, his archaic printing, his dreams of Sigurd and of Gudrun and of Guinevere, his essays on the unloveliness of our life and art...and his fierce anger against most things that we delight to honour." In a letter to Andreas Scheu dated September 5, 1883, Morris recalled:

We found that all the minor arts were in a state of complete degradation, especially in England, and accordingly in 1861, with the conceited courage of a young man, I set myself to reforming all that and started a sort of firm for producing decorative articles...and we made some progress before long, though we were naturally much ridiculed.

ON THE BEAUTY OF NATURAL FORMS, MOTIFS AND MATERIALS

For everything made by man's hands has a form, which must either be beautiful or ugly; beautiful if it is in accord with Nature, and helps her; ugly if it is discordant with Nature, and thwarts her; it cannot be indifferent.

🌿   🌿   🌿

Now it is one of the chief uses of decoration, the chief part of its alliance with nature, that it has to sharpen our dulled senses in this matter: for this end are those wonders of intricate patterns interwoven, those strange forms invented, which men have so long delighted in: forms and intricacies that do not necessarily imitate nature, but in which the hand of the craftsman is guided to work in the way that she does, till the web, the cup, or the knife, look as natural, nay as lovely, as the green field, the river bank, or the mountain flint.

"The Lesser Arts," lecture, December 1877

I was at Kelmscott the other day, and betwixt fishing, I cut a handful of poplar twigs and boiled them, and dyed a lock of wool a very good yellow...

🌿   🌿   🌿

For a great heap of skein-wool has come for me and more is coming: and yesterday evening we set our blue-vat the last thing before coming here. I should have liked you to see the charm work on it: we dyed a lock of wool bright blue in it, and left the liquor a clear primrose colour.

Letters (on the beauty of natural dyes)

Those natural forms which are at once most familiar and most delightful to us, as well from association as from beauty, are the best for our purpose. The rose, the lily, the tulip, the oak, the vine, and all the herbs and trees that even we cockneys know about, they will serve our turn.

Try to get the most out of your material, but always in such a way as honours it most. Not only should it be obvious what your material is, but something should be done with it which is specially natural to it, something that could not be done with any other. This is the very *raison d'être* of decorative art: to make stone look like ironwork, or wood like silk, or pottery like stone is the last resource of the decrepitude of art.

Some Hints on Pattern Designing, *1881*

However original a man may be, he cannot afford to disregard the works of art that have been produced in times past when design was flourishing; he is bound to study old examples, but he is also bound to supplement that by a careful study of nature, because if he does not he will certainly fall into a sort of cut and dried, conventional method of designing.

Address before the Royal Commission
for Technical Instruction, 1882

I have tried to produce goods which are genuine as far as their mere substances are concerned, and should have on that account the primary beauty in them which belongs to naturally treated substances; have tried, for instance, to make woollen substances as woollen as possible, cotton as cotton as possible and so on; I have only the dyes which are natural and simple.

Interview in The Clarion, *1892*

Never forget the material you are working with, and try always to use it for what it can do best: if you feel yourself hampered with the material in which you are working, instead of being helped by it, you have so far not learned your business. The special limitations of the material should be a pleasure to you, not a hindrance: a designer, therefore, should always thoroughly understand the processes of the special manufacture of the material he is dealing with.

The meaningless stripes and spots and other tormentings of the simple twill of the web, which are so common in the woven ornament of the eighteenth century and in our times, should be carefully avoided: all these things are the last resource of a jaded invention and a contempt of the simple and fresh beauty that comes of a sympathetic suggestion of natural forms: if the pattern be vigorously and firmly drawn with a true feeling for the beauty of line and *silhouette*, the play of light and shade on the material of the simple twill will give all the necessary variety.

Owing to the comparative coarseness of the work, the designs should always be very elementary in form and suggestive merely of forms of leafage, flowers, beasts and birds, etc. The soft graduations of tint to which tapestry lends itself are unfit for carpet-weaving: beauty and variety of colour must be attained by harmonious juxtaposition of tints.

Last of the methods of ornamenting cloth comes Embroidery: of the design of which it must be said that one of its aims should be the exhibition of beautiful material. Furthermore, it is not worth doing unless it is either very copious and rich, or very delicate—or both.

"Textiles," article, 1893

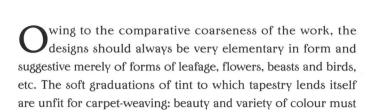

ON   CRAFTSMANSHIP
AND   CREATIVITY

Y ou may be sure that any decoration is futile, and has fallen into at least the first stage of degradation, when it does not remind you of something beyond itself, of something of which it is but a visible symbol.

Lecture, 1881

M y view is that it is not desirable to divide the labour between the artist and what is technically called the designer, and I think it desirable on the whole that the artist and designer should practically be one.

1882

T hese arts...are the sweeteners of human labour, both to the handicraftsman, whose life is spent in working in them, and to people in general who are influenced by the sight of them at every turn of the day's work: they make our toil, our rest fruitful.

"The Lesser Arts," lecture, December 1877

History (so called) has remembered the kings and warriors, because they destroyed; Art has remembered the people, because they created.

"The Art of the People," lecture, 1879

Whereas all works of craftsmanship were once beautiful, unwittingly or not, they are now divided into two kinds, works of art and non-works of art: now nothing made by man's hands can be indifferent: it must either be beautiful and elevating, or ugly and degrading.

"The Beauty of Life," lecture, 1880

I believe machines can do everything, except make works of art.

"Art and the Beauty of Earth," lecture, 1881

Hold fast to distinct form in art. Don't think too much of style, but set yourself to get out of you what you think beautiful, and express it, as cautiously as you please, but quite distinctly, and without vagueness. You must see it before you can draw it, whether the design be of your own invention or nature's. Remember always, form before colour, and outline, silhouette, before modelling; not because these latter are of less importance, but because they can't be right if the first are wrong.

Ornamental patternwork, to be raised above the contempt of reasonable men, must possess three qualities: beauty, imagination, and order.

     🌿   🌿   🌿

Every work of man which has beauty in it must have some meaning also; that the presence of any beauty in a piece of handicraft implies that the mind of the man who made it was more or less excited at the time, was lifted somewhat above the commonplace, that he had something to communicate to his fellows which they did not know or feel before, and which they would never have known or felt if he had not been there to force them to it.

     🌿   🌿   🌿

Rational growth is necessary to all patterns...Take heed in this growth that each member of it be strong and crisp, that the lines do not get thready or flabby or too far from their stock to sprout firmly and vigorously; even where a line ends it should look as if it had plenty of capacity for more growth if so it would.

Some Hints on Pattern Designing, *1881*

These, then are the first conditions of good glass painting as we perceive them—well-balanced and shapely figures, pure and simple drawing, and a minimum of light and shade. After this we ask for beautiful colour....Colour, pure and sweet, is the least you should ask for in a painted window.

1883

The aim should be to combine clearness of form and firmness of structure with the mystery which comes of abundance and richness of detail...Do not introduce any lines or objects which cannot be explained by the structure of the pattern; it is just this logical sequence of form...which prevents the eye wearying of the repetition of the pattern...Do not be afraid of large patterns.

Above all things, avoid vagueness; run any risk of failure rather than involve yourselves in a tangle of poor weak lines that people can't make out. Definite form bounded by firm outline is a necessity for all ornament.

Lecture, 1888

The noblest of the weaving arts is Tapestry, in which there is nothing mechanical: it may be looked upon as a mosaic of pieces of colour made up of dyed threads, and is capable of producing wall ornament of any degree of elaboration within the proper limits of duly considered decorative work.

"Textiles," article, 1893

ON ART AND SOCIETY

I believe that art has such sympathy with cheerful freedom, open-heartedness and reality so much she sickens under selfishness and luxury; that she will not live thus isolated and exclusive. I will go further than this and say that on such terms I do not wish her to live...I do not want art for a few, any more than education for a few, or freedom for a few.

🌿   🌿   🌿

To give people pleasure in the things they must perforce use, that is one great office of decoration; to give people pleasure in the things they must perforce make, that is the other use of it.

🌿   🌿   🌿

Nothing can be a work of art which is not useful; that is to say, which does not minister to the body when well under command of the mind, or which does not amuse, soothe, or elevate the mind in a healthy state.

🌿   🌿   🌿

Tomorrow, ...the civilized world, no longer greedy, strifeful, and destructive, shall have a new art, a glorious art, made by the people and for the people, as a happiness to the maker and user.

🌿   🌿   🌿

The necessary workaday furniture...should, of course, be well made and well proportioned, but simple to the last degree. But besides this type of furniture, there is the kind I should call state furniture. I mean sideboards, cabinets, and the like, which we have quite as much for beauties' sake as for use; we need not spare ornament on these, but may make them as elegant and elaborate as we can with carving, inlaying, or painting; these are the blossoms of the art of furniture.

"The Lesser Arts," lecture, December 1877

If you want a golden rule that will fit everybody, this is it: *Have nothing in your houses that you do not know to be useful, or believe to be beautiful.*

Surely since we are Servants of a Cause, hope must be ever with us, and sometimes perhaps it will so quicken our vision that it will outrun the slow lapse of time, and show us the victorious days when millions of those who now sit in darkness will be enlightened by an Art made by people and for the people.

"The Beauty of Life," lecture, 1880

In spite of all the success I have had, I have not failed to be conscious that the art I have been helping to produce would fall with the death of a few of us who really care about it, that a reform in art which is founded on individualism must perish with the individuals who have set it going. Both my historical studies and my practical conflict with the philistinism of modern society have *forced* on me the conviction that art cannot have a real life and growth under the present system of commercialism and profit-mongering.

Letter to Andreas Scheu, 1883

I have got to understand thoroughly the manner of work under which the art of the Middle Ages was done, and that that is the *only* manner of work which can turn out popular art, only to discover that it is impossible to work in that manner in this profit-grinding society.

Clarion, *1892*

When an artist has really a very keen sense of beauty, I venture to think that he can not literally represent an event that takes place in modern life. He must add something or other to qualify or soften the ugliness and sordidness of the surroundings of life in our generation. That is not only the case with pictures...it is the case also in literature...By all means, if anyone is really moved by the spirit to treat modern subjects, let him do so...but...I don't think he has a right, under the circumstances and considering the evasions he is absolutely bound to make, to lay any blame on his brother artist who turns back again to the life of past times; or, who, shall we rather say, since his imagination must have some garb or another, naturally takes the raiment of some period in which the surroundings of life were not ugly but beautiful.

Lecture, 1891

To sum, up, then, the study of history and the love and practice of art forced me into a hatred of the civilization which, if things were to stop as they are, would turn history into inconsequent nonsense, and make art a collection of the curiosities of the past, which would have no serious relation to the life of the present.

"How I Became a Socialist"
Article written for Justice, *1894*

And there the number of them that were sealed: and there were sealed an hundred and forty and four thousand of all the tribes of the Children of Israel

Abel · Davit · Isaiah · S Peter · S Paul · S Austin · S Catherine

Abraham · Moses · Eve · S Matt · S Mary Magdalene · S John · S Agnes · S Alban

AESTHETICS
IN
LIVING SPACE

Architecture and Environment

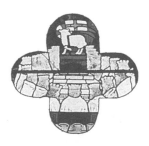

On leaving Oxford, Morris, who had been destined for a career in the church, instead declared his intention of becoming an architect and became an articled apprentice. His talents and interests were soon to lead him in other directions, but he nevertheless exerted tremendous influence over domestic English architecture during his lifetime. In 1877 he founded the Society for the Protection of Ancient Buildings (which he nicknamed the "Anti-Scrape Society") to protest against the destructive policy of the restoration of churches and other historical buildings. While his Socialist principles caused him to muse on the model factory and home, it was in the Red House at Bexley in Kent, which he commissioned Philip Webb to design, that his architectural ideal became manifest: "A new kind of life opened up vaguely before him, in which 'that small palace of art of my own' long recognised by him as one of his besetting dreams was now peopled with the forms of life and children, and contracted to the limits of some actual home, in which life and its central purposes need not be thwarted by any basis of ugliness of immediate surroundings." (J. W. Mackail, *The Life of William Morris,* 1899.)

ON MEDIEVAL
ARCHITECTURE

 27

He [Walter Scott] thought himself continually bound to seem to feel ashamed of, and to excuse himself for, his love of Gothic Architecture: he felt that it was romantic, and he knew that it gave him pleasure, but somehow he had not found out that it was art, having been taught in many ways that nothing can be art that was not done by a named man under academical rules.

"The Beauty of Life," lecture, 1880

Consider London of the fourteenth century: a smallish town, beautiful from one end to the other; streets of low white-washed houses with a big Gothic church standing in the middle of it; a town surrounded by walls, with a forest of church towers and spires, besides the cathedral and the abbeys and priories; every one of the houses in it, nay, every shed, bearing in it a certain amount of absolute, definite, distinct, conscientious art. Think of the difference between that and the London of to-day.

Just consider what England was in the fourteenth century. The population...at about four millions. Think then of the amount of beautiful and dignified buildings which those four millions built...Not only those churches and houses which we see, but also those which have been destroyed...Those buildings...contained much art: pictures, metal-work, carvings, tapestry, and the like, altogether forming a prodigious mass of art, produced by a scanty population. Try to imagine that.

Address to the Anti-Scrape Society, 1889

It seems pitiable indeed that the most important documents of all, the ancient buildings of the Middle Ages, the work of associated labour and thought of the *people,* the result of a chain of tradition unbroken from the earliest stages of art, should be falsified by an uneasy desire to do something, a vulgar craving for formal completeness, which is almost essentially impossible in a building that has grown from decade to decade and century to century.

Letter to the Editor, The Daily Chronicle,
October 1, 1895

ON PRESERVATION

We urge [society] to treat our ancient buildings as monuments of a bygone art, created by bygone manners, that modern art cannot meddle with without destroying.

> The Manifesto of the Society for the
> Protection of Ancient Buildings, *1877*

St. Mark's, Venice, has now become a work of art, a monument of history, and a piece of nature.

> *Letter to the Editor,* The Daily News, *October 31, 1879*

Sir:

My eye just now caught the word 'restoration' in the morning paper, and, on looking closer, I saw that this time it is nothing less than the minster of Tewkesbury that is to be destroyed by Sir Gilbert Scott. Is it altogether too late to do something to save it—it and what ever else of beautiful or historical is still left us on the sites of the ancient buildings we were once so famous for? Would it not be of some use once for all, and with the least delay possible, to set on foot an association for the purpose of watching over and protecting these relics?

> *Letter, 1877*

Thus the matter stands: these old buildings have been altered and added to century after century, often beautifully, always historically; their very value, a great part of it, lay in that...But of late years a great uprising of ecclesiastical zeal, coinciding with a great increase of study, and consequently of knowledge of mediaeval architecture, has driven people into spending their money on these buildings, not merely with the purpose of repairing them, of keeping them safe, clean, and wind and water-tight, but also of 'restoring' them to some ideal state of perfection; sweeping away if possible all signs of what had befallen them at least since the Reformation, and often since dates much earlier: this has sometimes been done with much disregard of art and entirely from ecclesiastical zeal, but oftener it has been well enough meant as regards art: yet...this restoration must be as impossible to bring about, as the attempt at it is destructive...I scarcely like to think what a great part of them have been made nearly useless to students of art and history.

"The Lesser Arts," lecture, 1877

Surely an opulent city, the capital of the commercial world, can afford some small sacrifice to spare these beautiful buildings the little plots of ground upon which they stand. Is it absolutely necessary that every scrap of space in the City should be devoted to money-making, and are religion, sacred memorials, recollections of the great dead, memorials of the past, works of England's greatest architect, to be banished from this wealthy City?

Letter to the editor, The Times, *1878*

I love art, and I love history, but it is living art and living history that I love. If we have no hope for the future, I do not see how we can look back on the past with pleasure. If we are to be less than men in time to come, let us forget that we have ever been men. It is in the interest of living art and living history that I oppose so-called restoration. What history can there be in a building bedaubed with ornament, which cannot at the best be anything but a hopeless and lifeless imitation for the hope and vigour of the earlier world?...Let us leave the dead alone, and, ourselves living, build for the living and those that shall live.

 31

Lecture, 1882

Our ancient architecture bears witness to the development of man's ideas, to the continuity of history, and, so doing, affords never-ceasing instruction, nay education, to the passing generations, not only telling us what were the aspirations of men passed away, but also what he may hope for in the time to come.

Lecture, 1884

Aⁿd the house itself was a fit guardian for all the beauty of this heart of summer.

🌼 🌼 🌼

The extravagant love of ornament which I had noted in this people elsewhere seemed here to have given place to the feeling that the house itself and its associations was the ornament of the country life amidst which it had been left stranded from old times, and that to reornament it would but take away its use as a piece of natural beauty.

News from Nowhere, *1891*

ON DEHUMANISING INDUSTRIALISATION

Though many of us love architecture dearly, and believe that it helps the healthiness both of body and soul to live among beautiful things, we of the big towns are mostly compelled to live in houses which have become a by-word of contempt for their ugliness and inconvenience. The stream of civilization is against us, and we cannot battle against it.

"The Lesser Arts," lecture, December 1877

Beginning by making their factories, buildings and sheds decent and convenient like their homes, they would infallibly go on to make them not merely negatively good, inoffensive merely, but even beautiful, so that the glorious art of architecture, now for some time slain by commercial greed, would be born again and flourish.

"The Beauty of Life," lecture, 1880

[Of a well-designed factory:]
There would be no serious difficulty in making them beautiful, as every building might be which serves its purpose duly, which is built generously as regards material, and which is built with pleasure by the builders and designers.

"How We Live and How We Might Live,"
article, Art and Socialism, 1887

DREAMER
OF
DREAMS 🌿

Poetry
and
Literature

At Oxford Morris discovered his interest in, and talent for, writing poetry. His first published work was *The Defence of Guenevere, and Other Poems* (1858), and this was followed by numerous romantic poems and stories, as well as Norse-style epics like *Sigurd the Volsung* (1876) and *The Earthly Paradise* (1868–70).

As his Socialist convictions became more profound, he worked his political beliefs into such poems as *A Dream of John Ball* (1888), for, as his biographer, J. W. Mackail, observed in 1899: "The idea that poetry could, or should, be cultivated as an isolated and specific product, or that towards its production it was desirable to isolate one's self from common interests and occupations, and stand a little apart from all the turmoils or trivialities of common life, was one which he found not so much untrue as unintelligible. 'If a chap can't compose an epic poem while he's weaving tapestry,' he once said, 'he had better shut up, he'll never do any good at all.'" (J. W. Mackail, *The Life of William Morris,* 1899.)

Morris was also committed to restoring beauty and quality to book design and production. He created his own typefaces and published fifty-three books at his Kelmscott Press, founded in Hammersmith, West London, in 1890. Special inks and paper contributed to the elegance of his monochrome art books, many of them designed by Edward Burne-Jones, which were published in limited editions for a discriminating market.

> Remember me a little then, I pray,
> The idle singer of an empty day.
> —*The Earthly Paradise (*1868–70)

FROM *THE EARTHLY PARADISE*

An Apology

Dreamer of dreams, born out of my due time,
Why should I strive to set the crooked straight?
Let it suffice me that my murmuring rhyme
Beats with light wing against the ivory gate,
Telling a tale not too importunate
To those who in the sleepy region stay,
Lulled by the singer of an empty day.

Folk say, a wizard to a northern king
At Christmas-tide such wondrous things did show,
That through one window men beheld the spring,
And through another saw the summer glow,
And through a third the fruited vines a-row,
While still unheard, but in its wonted way,
Piped the drear wind of that December day.

So with this Earthly Paradise it is,
If ye will read aright, and pardon me,
Who strive to build a shadowy isle of bliss
Midmost the beating of the steely sea,
Where tossed about all hearts of men must be;
Whose ravening monsters mighty men must slay,
Not the poor singer of an empty day.

from **Prologue: The Wanderers**

A damsel knelt, praying in words so sweet
For what I know not now, that both mine eyes
Grew full of tears, and I must bid her rise
And sit beside me; step by step she came
Up the gold stair, setting my heart a-flame
With all her beauty, till she reached the throne
And there sat down, but as with her alone
In that vast hall, my hand her hand did seek,
And on my face I felt her balmy cheek,
Throughout my heart there shot a dreadful pang.

Forget six counties overhung with smoke,
Forget the snorting steam and piston stroke,
Forget the spreading of the hideous town;
Think rather of the pack-horse on the down,
And dream of London, small and white and clean,
The clear Thames bordered by its gardens green.

from **November**

Yea, I have looked, and seen November there;
The changeless seal of change it seemed to be,
Fair death of things that, living once, were fair;
Bright sign of loneliness too great for me,
Strange image of the dread eternity,
In whose void patience how can these have part,
These outstretched feverish hands, this restless heart?

from **The Man Who Never Laughed Again**

A h, these, with life so done with now, might deem
   That better is it resting in a dream,
Yea, e'en a dull dream, than with outstretched hand,
And wild eyes, face to face with life to stand...
Than waking in a hard taskmaster's grasp
Because we strove the unsullied joy to clasp—
Than just to find our hearts the world, as we
Still though we were and ever longed to be,
To find nought real except ourselves, and find
All care for all things scattered to the wind,
Scarce in our hearts the very pain alive.
Compelled to breathe indeed, compelled to strive,
Compelled to fear, yet not allowed to hope—

VERSES AND
REFLECTIONS

Summer Night

O love, O love, though thy lids are shut close,
Yet hearken the sweet-breathed rustling rose!

Why liest thou sleeping, yet red with shame
While the harp-strings tremble to hear thy name?

Hearken the harp in a trembling hand!
Hearken soft speech of a far off land!

O my love, if thou hearest my foot-steps anear
Thy very breathing methinks I may hear

O my sweet, is it true that we are alone,
The grey leaves a-quiver twixt us and the moon

O me, the love, the love in thine eyes,
Now the night is a-dying as all life dies!

Art thou come, swift end of beginning of bliss?
O my sweet! O thine eyes, O thy hands, O thy kiss!

from **Praise of My Lady**

M y lady seems of ivory
Forehead, straight nose and cheeks that be
Hollow'd a little mournfully.
  —Beata mea Domina!

Her great eyes, standing far apart,
Draw up some memory from her heart,
And gaze out very mournfully;
  —Beata mea Domina!

So beautiful and kind they are,
But most times looking out afar,
Waiting for something, not for me.
  —Beata mea Domina!

I wonder if the lashes long
Are those that do her bright eyes wrong,
for always half tears seem to be
  —Beata mea Domina!

Lurking below the underlid,
Darkening the place where they lie hid—
If they should rise and flow for me!
  Beata mea Domina!
        Written for Jane Burden, during their courtship

Prologue to *The Volsung Tale*

O hearken ye who speak the English Tongue,
How in a waste land ages long ago—
The very heart of the North—bloomed into song
After long brooding o'er this tale of woe!
Hearken, and marvel, how it might be so,
How such a sweetness so well crowned could be
Betwixt the ice-hills and the cold grey sea

Nay rather, marvel not thou those should cling
Unto the thought of great lives past away,
Whom God has stripped so bare of everything
Save the one longing to wear through their day
In fearless wise; the hope the Gods to stay,
When at that last tide gathered wrong and hate
Shall meet blind yearning on the fields of fate.

Yea, in the first grey dawning of our race
This ruth-crowned tangle to sad hearts was dear.
Then rose a seeming sun, the lift gave place,
Unto a seeming heaven, far-off but clear;
But that passed too, and afternoon is here;
Nor was the morn so fruitful or so long
But we may hearken when ghosts moan of wrong.

For as amid the clatter of the town
When eve comes on with unabated noise,
The soaring wind will sometimes drop adown
And bear unto our chamber the sweet voice
Of bells, that mid the swallows do rejoice
Half heard to amke us sad; so we awhile
With echoed grief like's tumult may beguile.

Naught vague, naught base our tale, that seems to say:
Be wide-eyed, kind, curse not the hand that smites
Curse not the kindness of a past good day,
Or hope of love: cast by all earth's delights
For very Love: through weary days and nights.
Abide thou, striving, howsoe'er in vain,
The inmost love of one more heart to gain.

So draw ye round and hearken, English Folk
Unto the best tale pity ever wrought,
Of how from dark to dark bright Sigurd broke
Of Brynhild's glorious soul by love distraught,
Of Gudrun's weary wandering unto naught
Of utter Love defeated utterly
Of Grief too strong to give Love time to die.

Love and Death

In the white-flowered hawthorn brake
Love be merry for my sake;
Twine the blossoms in my hair
Kiss me where I am most fair
Kiss me, sweet, for who knoweth
What thing cometh after death!

Nay, thy garlanded gold hair
Hides thee where thou art most fair,
Hides the rose-tinged hills of snow—
O my love I hold thee now!
Kiss me, sweet, for who knoweth
What thing cometh after death!

Shall we weep for a dead day,
Or set sorrow in our way?
Hidden in my golden hair
Wilt thou weep that the days wear?
Kiss me, sweet, for who knoweth
What thing cometh after death!

Weep, O love, the days that fly
Now, while I can feel thy breath,
Then may I remember it
Sad and old, and near my death
Kiss me sweet, for who knoweth
What thing cometh after death!

From this dull rainy undersky and low,
This murky ending of a leaden day,
That never knew the sun, this half-thawed snow,
These tossing black boughs faint against the grey
Of gathering night, thou turnest, dear, away
Silent, but with thy scarce-seen kindly smile
Sent through the dusk my longing to beguile.

c. 1868

 45

O why and for what are we waiting? while our brothers
droop and die,
And on every wind of the heavens a wasted life goes by.

How long shall they reproach us where crowd on crowd they
dwell,
Poor ghosts of the wicked city, the gold-crushed hungry hell?

Through squalid life they laboured, in sordid grief they died,
Those sons of a mighty mother, those props of England's
pride.

from Chants for Socialists, *1883*

from **March of the Workers**

Hark the rolling of the thunder!
Lo the sun! and lo, thereunder
Riseth wrath, and hope, and wonder,
And the host comes marching on.

The singers have sung and the builders have builded,
The painters have fashioned their tales of delight;
For what and for whom hath the world's book been gilded,
When all is for these but the blackness of night?
> *from The Message of the March Wind*
> *The Pilgrims of Hope,* 1885

I am old and have seen
Many things that have been;
Both grief and peace
And wane and increase.
No tale I tell
Of ill or well,
But this I say,
Night treadeth on day,
And for worst and best
Right good is rest.
> *1891*

L ove is enough: draw near and behold me
    Ye who pass by the way to your rest and your laughter,
  And are full of the hope of the dawn coming after;
For the strong of the world have bought me and sold me
  And my house is all wasted from threshold to rafter,
  —Pass by me, and hearken, and think of me not!

Ye know not how void is your hope and your living:
  Depart with your helping lest yet ye undo me!
  Ye know not that at nightfall she draweth near to me,
There is soft speech between us and words of forgiving
  Till in dead of the midnight her kisses thrill through me.
  —Pass by me and hearken, and waken me not!
     1891

ON THE
LITERARY ARTS

The verse would come easy enough if only I had a subject which would fill my heart and mind: but to write verse for the sake of writing it is a crime in a man of my years and experience.

Letter to Georgiana Burne-Jones, October 13, 1879

Out of all despair sprang a new time of hope lighted by the torch of the French Revolution: and all things that have languished with the languishing of art, rose afresh and surely heralded its new birth: in good earnest poetry was born again, and the English Language, which under the hands of sycophantic verse-makers had been reduced to a miserable jargon, whose meaning, if it have a meaning, cannot be made out without translation, flowed clear, pure, and simple, along with the music of Blake and Coleridge.

❧   ❧   ❧

With that literature in which romance, that is to say humanity, was re-born, there sprang up also a feeling for the romance of external nature...joined with a longing to know something real of the lives of those who have gone before us.

"The Beauty of Life," lecture, 1880

I began printing books with the hope of producing some which would have a definite claim to beauty, while at the same time they should be easy to read and should not dazzle the eye, or trouble the intellect of the reader by eccentricity of form in the letters. And it was the essence of my undertaking to produce books which it would be a pleasure to look upon as pieces of printing and arrangements of type.

> *"A Note by William Morris on his Aims
> in Founding the Kelmscott Press"*

A work of utility might also be a work of art, if we cared to make it so.

> *"Printing,"* Arts and Crafts Essays, *1893*

The
Ideal
Society

I n his artistic endeavors, one of Morris's abiding obsessions was a hatred of industrialisation: "[I] love art and manufactures, & hate commerce and moneymaking more than ever" [letter to Rosalind Francis Howard, July 30, 1875]. It became clear to him that the conditions which the working classes endured were unacceptable, both in physical terms, and in the suppression of *joie de vivre*. In 1883 he joined the Social Democratic Federation; in 1884, when the Federation broke up, Morris—a member of the artistic élite—led the Socialist League and campaigned vociferously for human equality. A contemporary explained this apparent anomaly: "That the 'idle singer of an empty day' should voice the claims and hopes of labour, stand up for the rights of free speech in Trafalgar Square, and speak from a waggon in Hyde Park, may have surprised those who only knew him upon one side; but to those who fully apprehended the reality, ardour, and sincerity of his nature, such action was but its logical outcome and complement, and assuredly it redounds to the honour of the artist, the scholar, and the poet whose loss we mourn today, that he was also a man." (Walter Crane's posthumous tribute to Morris in *Progressive Review,* November 1896)

> *Luxury cannot exist without slavery of some kind or other, and its abolition will be blessed...by the freeing both of the slaves and of their masters.*

ON EXISTING EVILS

For ever must the rich man hate the poor.

"Bellerophon at Argos," The Earthly Paradise

While we are met here...to further the spread of education in art, Englishmen in India are...actively destroying the very sources of that education—jewellery, metalwork, pottery, calico-printing, brocade-weaving, carpet-making—all the famous and historical arts of the great peninsula have been...thrust aside for the advantage of any paltry scrap of so-called commerce.

"The Art of the People," lecture, 1879

Ibegin to doubt if civilization itself may not be sometimes so much adulterated as scarcely to be worth the carrying—anyhow it cannot be worth much, when it is necessary to kill a man in order to make him accept it.

Lecture, 1880

Civilization...has let one wrong and tyranny grow and swell into this, that a few have no work to do, and are therefore unhappy, the many have degrading work to do, and are therefore unhappy...Of all countries ours is...the most masterful, the most remorseless, in pushing forward this blind civilization....For our parts, we think that the remedy is to be found in the simplification of life, and the curbing of luxury and the desires for tyranny and mastery that it gives birth to.

I had thought that civilization meant the attainment of peace and order and freedom, of goodwill between man and man, of the love of truth and the hatred of injustice...a life free from craven fear, but full of incident: that was what I thought it meant, not more stuffed chairs and more cushions, and more carpets and gas, and more dainty meat and drink—and therewithal more and sharper differences between class and class.

If civilization is to go no further than this, it had better not have gone so far: if it does not aim at getting rid of this misery and giving some share in the happiness and dignity of life to *all* the people that it has created...it is simply an organized injustice, a mere instrument for oppression, so much the worse than that which has gone before it, as its pretensions are higher, its slavery subtler, its mastery harder to overthrow, because supported by such a dense mass of commonplace well-being and comfort.

"The Beauty of Life," lecture, 1880

In looking into matters social and political I have but one rule, that in thinking of the condition of any body of men I shall ask myself, 'How could you bear it yourself? what would you feel if you were poor against the system under which you live?' I have always been uneasy when I had to ask myself that question, and of late years I have had to ask it so often, that I have seldom had it out of my mind: and the answer to it has more and more made me ashamed of my own position, and more and more made me feel that if I had not been born rich or well-to-do I should have found my position unendurable....Nothing can argue me out of this feeling, which I say plainly is a matter of religion to me: the contrasts of rich and poor are unendurable and ought not to be endured by either rich or poor.

I do not believe in the world being saved by any system,—I only assert the necessity of attacking systems grown corrupt, and no longer leading anywhither: that to my mind is the case with the present system of capital and labour. I have personally been gradually driven to the conclusion that art has been handcuffed by it, and will die out of civilization if the system lasts.

Letter to C. E. Maurice, July 1, 1883

Once again I tell you that our present system is not so much a confusion...as a tyranny: one and all of us in some way or other we are drilled to the service of Commercial War; if our individual aspirations or capacities do not fit in with it, so much the worse for them: the iron service of the capitalist will not bear the loss, the individual must; everything must give way to this; nothing can be done if a profit cannot be made of it: it is for this that we are overworked, are made to fear starvation, live in hovels, are herded...into foul places called towns...it is for this that we let half Scotland be depopulated...and turn its stout peasants and herdsmen into mere flunkies of idle fools: it is for this that we let our money, our name, our power, be used to drag off poor wretches from our pinched fields and our dreadful slums, to kill and be killed in a cause they know nothing of.

"Commercial War," lecture

I have noted of late years a growing impatience on the part of the more luxurious portion of society of the amusements and habits of the workers, when they in any way interfere with the calm of their luxury; or to put it in plainer language a tendency to arrogant petty tyranny in these matters. They would, if they could, clear the streets of everything that may injure their delicate susceptibilities...They would clear the streets of costermongers, organs, processions, and lecturers of all kinds, and make them a sort of decent prison corridors, with people just trudging to and from their work.

"Free Speech in the Streets," article,
Commonweal, *1886*

The ideas which have taken hold of me will not let me rest: nor can I see anything else worth thinking of. How can it be otherwise, when to me society, which to many seems an orderly arrangement for allowing decent people to get through their lives creditably and with some pleasure, seems mere cannibalism; nay worse...is grown so corrupt, so steeped in hypocrisy and lies, that one turns from one stratum of it to another with hopeless loathing.

Letter to Georgiana Burne-Jones, 1886

I have pondered all these things, and how men fight and lose the battle, and the thing that they fought for comes about in spite of their defeat, and when it comes turns out not to be what they meant, and other men have to fight for what they meant under another name.

A Dream of John Ball, *1888*

A part from the desire to produce beautiful things, the leading passion of my life has been and is hatred of modern civilization. What shall I say concerning its mastery of and its waste of mechanical power, its commonwealth so poor, its enemies of the commonwealth so rich, its stupendous organization—for the misery of life! Its contempt of simple pleasures, which everyone could enjoy but for its folly? Its eyeless vulgarity which has destroyed art, the one certain solace of labour?

Article written for Justice, 1894
"How I became a Socialist"

UTOPIA REVISITED

The reward of labour is life.

That thing which I understand by real art is the expression by man of his pleasure in labour. I do not believe he can be happy in his labour without expressing that happiness; and especially is this so when he is at work at anything in which he specially excels.

   ❧   ❧   ❧

It is the hope of my life that this may one day be changed; that popular art may grow again in our midst; that we may have an architectural style, the growth of its own times, but connected with all history.

   ❧   ❧   ❧

How can you really educate men who lead the life of machines, who only think for the few hours during which they are not at work, who in short spend almost all their lives in doing work which is not proper for developing them body and mind in some worthy way? You cannot educate, you cannot civilize men, unless you can give them a share in art.

   ❧   ❧   ❧

The working class, the 'residuum' of modern civilization, the terror of radical politicians, and the tool of reactionists, will become the great mass of orderly thinking people, sweet and fair in its manners, and noble in its aspirations, and that...is the sole hope of worthy, living, enduring art: nothing else, I say, will help.

Lectures, 1879–80

I think of a country where every man has work enough to do, and no one has too much: where no man has to work himself stupid in order to be just able to live: where on the contrary it will be easy for a man to live if he will but work, impossible if he will not...where everyman's work would be pleasant to himself and helpful to his neighbour; and then his leisure...(of which he ought to have plenty) would be thoughtful and rational.

1880

I will now let my claims for decent life stand as I have made them:...First, a healthy body; second, an active mind in sympathy with the past, present, and the future; thirdly, occupation fit for a healthy body and an active mind; and fourthly, a beautiful world to live in.

Article, Art and Socialism, *1887*
"How We Live and How We Might Live"

People living under the conditions of life above mentioned, having manual skill, technical and general education, and leisure to use these advantages, are quite sure to develop a love of art, that is to say, a sense of beauty and interest in life, which in the long run must stimulate them to the desire for artistic creation, the satisfaction of which is of all pleasures the greatest.

"A Factory As It Might Be," article, 1887

Fellowship is heaven, and lack of fellowship is hell: fellowship is life, and lack of fellowship is death: and the deeds that ye do upon the earth, it is for fellowship's sake that ye do them.

A Dream of John Ball, *1888*

Go on living while you may, striving with whatsoever pain and labour needs must be, to build up little by little the new day of fellowship, and rest, and happiness. If others can see it as I have seen it, then it may be called a vision rather than a dream.

News from Nowhere, *1891*

ON SOCIALISM

I do most earnestly desire that something more startling could be done than mere constant private grumbling and occasional public speaking to lift the standard of revolt against the sordidness which people are so stupid as to think necessary.

Letter to Georgiana Burne-Jones, 1880

On the genuineness and reality of that hope [for a Socialist society] the existence, the reason for existence of our Society [Anti-Scrape] depends. Believe me, it will not be possible for a small knot of cultivated people to keep alive an interest in the art and records of the past amidst the present conditions of a sordid and heart-breaking struggle for existence for the many, and a languid sauntering through life for the few. But when society is so reconstituted that all citizens will have a chance made up of due leisure and reasonable work, then will all society, and not our 'Society' only, resolve to protect ancient buildings...for then at last they will begin to understand that they are part of their present lives, and part of themselves.

Lecture, 1884

Here are two classes, face to face with each other...No man can exist in society and be neutral, no-body can be a mere looker on: one camp or another you have got to join: you must either be a reactionary and be crushed by the progress of the race, and help it that way: or you must join in the march of progress, trample down all opposition, and help it that way.

"Commercial War," lecture

Whatever Socialism may lead to, our aim...is to obtain for the whole people, duly organized, the possession and control of all the means of production and exchange, destroying at the same time all national rivalries.

Letter to Robert Thompson, July 24, 1884

How can we of the middle classes, we the capitalists, and our hangers-on, help the workers?...By renouncing our class, and on all occasions when antagonism rises up between the classes casting in our lot with the victims...There is no other way: and this way, I tell you plainly, will in the long run give us plenty of occasion for self-sacrifice.

We must do what we can, improve every opportunity, and like Quintus Fabius, who was never defeated, reform the government, not overthrow it. We must take the present social order and build upon it.

Defining the policy of the Fabian Society, 1884

I t is a new Society that we are working to realise, not a cleaning up of our present tyrannical muddle into an improved smoothly-working form of that same "order," a mass of dull and useless people organized into classes, amidst which the antagonism should be moderated and veiled so that they should act as checks on each other for the insurance of the stability of the system.

The real business of Socialists is to impress on the workers the fact that they are a class, whereas they ought to be Society; if we mix ourselves up with Parliament we shall confuse and dull this fact in people's minds instead of making it clear and intensifying it. The work that lies before us at present is to *make Socialists,* to cover the country with a network of associations composed of men who feel their antagonism to the dominant classes, and have no temptation to waste their time in the thousand follies of party politics.

Article, 1885

W hat is this, the sound and rumour? What is this that all men hear,
Like the wind in the hollow valleys when the storm is drawing near,
Like the rolling on of ocean in the eventide of fear?
'Tis the people marching on.

"The March of the Workers,"
Chants for Socialists, *1885.*

The mere fact that a body of men, however small, are banded together as Socialist missionaries shows that the change is going on. As the working-classes, the real organic part of society, take in these ideas, hope will arise in them, and they will claim changes in society, many of which will doubtless not tend directly towards their emancipation, because they will be claimed without due knowledge of the one thing necessary to claim, equality of condition; but which indirectly will help to break up our rotten sham society, while that claim for equality of condition will be made constantly and with growing loudness till it must be listened to, and then at last it will only be a step over the border, and the civilized world will be socialized; and, looking back at what has been, we shall be astonished to think of how long we submitted to live as we live now.

Article, Art and Socialism, *1887*
"How We Live and How We Might Live"

What I mean by Socialism is a condition of society in which there should be neither rich or poor, neither master nor master's man, neither idle nor overworked, neither brain-sick workers nor heart-sick workers, in a word, in which all men would be living in equality of condition, and would manage their affairs unmasterfully, and with the full consciousness that harm to one would mean harm to all—the realization at last of the meaning of the word commonwealth.

Article written for Justice, *1894*
"How I became a Socialist"